JAPANESE RECIPES

FROM

MARI'S TOKYO KITCHEN

MARI NAMESHIDA

JAPANESE RECIPES

FROM

MARI'S TOKYO KITCHEN

MARI NAMESHIDA

PIA Corporation
1-2-20, Higashi, Shibuya-ku, Tokyo, 150-0011 Japan
http://corporate.pia.jp/

Project coordination: Tomoko Kawai
Art Direction: Mitsunobu Hosoyamada [Hosoyamada Design Office]
Design: Yasuna Fujii [Hosoyamada Design Office]
Photography: Gaku Yamaya
Prop Styling: Makiko Iwasaki
English Editing: Noriko Yokota and Kelly Waldron
Hair & Make-up Tomoya Handa

First Edition, 2015

ISBN 978-4-8356-2844-8

This book is dedicated to my mother Chiharu Murakami,
my husband Ryo, and to everyone
who shares their hearts through home cooking.

Introduction

Japanese food is really not that difficult to prepare at home. There is a misconception that Japanese cuisine is complicated and consists of multiple courses. And some believe that Japanese cuisine is limited to simply sushi and tempura. In fact, I don't eat either of these things very often! At home, we enjoy simple meals, which usually include rice, miso soup, grilled fish, seasonal vegetables, and *natto*. At the heart of Japanese home cooking, like that of many other cultures, is the food prepared by our mothers.

In 2011, I enlisted the help of a friend to recruit some of his expat friends to be the first students in my English language cooking classes. Prior to that, I spent my time visiting over 30 countries on a quest to learn more about how people around the world cook at home. What I gathered from this experience was that the flavor of the foods prepared at home by mothers trumped any restaurant meal.

My students have been surprised by how different the dishes we prepare in class are from those that they have tried in restaurants. By using fresh local ingredients, they discover umami, unadulterated by excess salt. The smooth flavor of kombu dashi, the sweetness of the freshest fish, really, any dish made at home with great care will touch peoples' hearts.

I'm happiest when I receive email from my students telling me that they've prepared the Japanese dishes they learned in class for their friends and family back home. I'm also happy when my students discover that Japanese home cooking is a result of care and wanting to bring out the best flavor of each ingredient. Home cooking speaks to the terroir of place—its people, geography, seasons and ingredients. I hope you experience this joy as you prepare these dishes from Japan.

Mari Nameshida

Contents

1 Soy Sauce [Shoyu]

The number one Japanese pantry staple is made by fermenting soy beans and wheat with salt. Any naturally-brewed soy sauce will add flavor to your dishes, but Marunaka Shoyu brand is my favorite.

2 White Miso [Shiro-miso]

Among the many varieties of white miso, I prefer white miso from Kyoto for its richer, sweeter taste and recommend Yamari or Ishino brands. Combined with yellow miso, it makes a great soup.

3 Haccho Miso

A popular miso for making dengaku sauce, this intense, salty, and umami-rich miso is also a great addition to miso soup. Yamari and Kakukyu produce especially good *haccho* miso.

4 Organic Miso

I reserve use of Kurano Sato brand for special occasions. It is made with organically-grown soy beans, rice, and *koji* starter. The traditional, long fermentation process they employ is very rare and expensive.

INGREDIENT GLOSSARY

Listed below are pantry staples as well as gift suggestions that would make excellent *omiyage* (souvenirs) for your friends!

5 Rice Vinegar [Kome-su]

In Japan, most vinegars are either produced from rice (kome-su) or from grains (*kokumotsu-su*) consisting of fermented wheat, barley or corn. If you are a novice cook, it is better to stick with rice vinegar.

6 Sake

You may have seen sake in grocery stores that contains salt or other additives. Pure sake makes better dishes, and Fukuma-samune and Fukunishiki brands are reasonably priced and additive-free.

7 Mirin

Most mirin sold abroad is actually a "mirin-style" seasoning with added sugar. Actually, mirin is not a sugar syrup, but a naturally-fermented rice product. Taste Mikawa Mirin on its own, and you'll be able to tell the difference.

8 Sesame Oil [Goma-abura]

We use two types of sesame oil: a roasted variety and a freshly-pressed one, called *taihaku*. High-quality and popular brands are Maruhon, Takemoto Yushi and Iwai no Goma-abura.

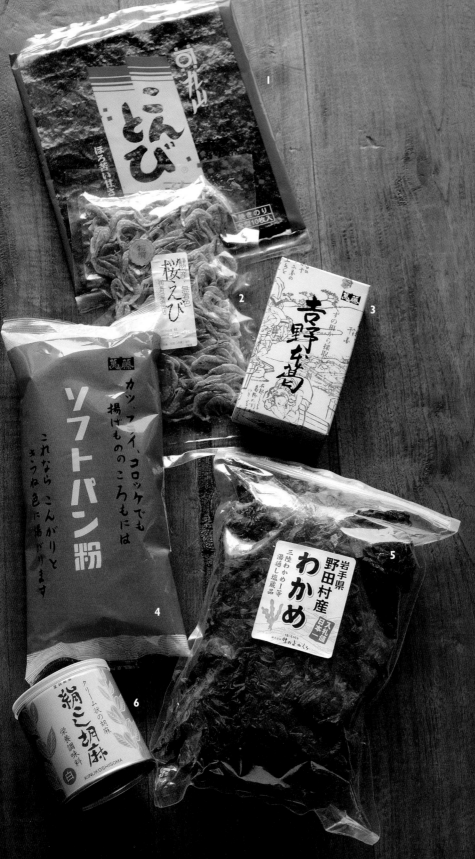

1 Nori

Nori comes in various shapes and sizes, and the flavor varies depending on where it was harvested. The most versatile size is *zenkei* (meaning "whole sheet"), about 20 cm / 8 in. square.

2 Sakura Shrimp [Sakura-ebi]

Japanese use dried shrimp like many other Asian countries, but *sakura* shrimp (sakura means cherry blossom) caught in Shizuoka lend a uniquely Japanese taste. If you are a fan of *kakiage* tempura, be sure to try this variety.

3 Kudzu

This is a relatively expensive root starch, comparable to arrowroot. It creates a smooth texture, is easily digested, and is often used in vegan recipes to set jellies, cakes, and other dishes.

4 Panko

Japanese-style bread crumbs that are essential for making tonkatsu and Japanese croquets. Panko is lighter and more flaky than regular bread crumbs, and makes extra-crispy fried dishes.

5 Wakame

Wakame is a type of seaweed often sold dried or salted for preservation. If you visit Tsukiji Market, make a stop at Aji no Yonekura. Their wakame is the best I've tasted, with a pleasant briny flavor.

6 Sesame Paste [Neri-goma]

Tahini is made of fresh sesame seeds ground into a paste, but Japanese *neri-goma* is made from roasted and ground sesame seeds. In addition to using it for sauces, I like to put it on my toast with honey to enjoy its nutty flavor.

MAKING STOCK [DASHI]

DASHI WITH KOMBU AND BONITO FLAKES

When you refer to dashi, it often indicates one made with kombu and bonito flakes. Dashi is between a stock and a broth, full of umami and smokiness from the bonito flakes. It keeps for three days in the refrigerator.

10 g dried kombu
20 g dried bonito flakes
1 L water

1 Gently wipe the kombu with a dry paper towel to remove impurities. Don't rinse with water, or the flavor will be lost.
2 Combine the water and the kombu in a pan and allow to soak for at least 30 minutes. Warm over low heat, and wait until the water reaches approximately 60°C / 140°F. The kombu will slowly float to the surface and tiny bubbles will appear. Remove the kombu. (The stock at this point is called kombu dashi and is used in some recipes without adding bonito flakes.) Maintain the temperature at 60°C / 140°F over very low heat for 10 minutes. If you have the time, you can poach the kombu for an hour to extract the most umami.
3 Turn up the heat and immediately add the bonito flakes. When the temperature reaches approximately 90°C /194°F, turn off the heat and lightly press the bonito flakes into the water with chopsticks.
4 Strain through a sieve lined with paper towels or cheesecloth. Don't squeeze the bonito flakes, or the dashi will have an off flavor.

DASHI WITH SHIITAKE MUSHROOMS

This is a vegetarian stock. Full of intense umami and natural sweetness. In Japan, it's often used to make tofu or vegetable dishes that appeal to even non-vegetarians. It keeps for two to three days in the refrigerator.

30 g dried shiitake mushrooms
1 L cold water

1 Lightly pat the shiitake mushrooms to remove impurities.
2 Combine the water and mushrooms in a bowl. Cover the surface of the water with plastic wrap so that all the mushrooms are submerged, and allow to soak in the refrigerator overnight.
Using tepid water expedites the process, but in order to extract the most umami, use cold water.
3 Strain through a sieve lined with paper towels to remove any small particles of dirt.

*The reconstituted shiitake mushrooms can be used as an ingredient. Cut into strips for miso soup or sautéed vegetables, or chop up for croquet filling.
*For a richer taste, simmer the reconstituted shiitake mushrooms with the stock in a pan over medium heat for several minutes. Strain well.

UNDERSTANDING KOMBU VARIETIES

The taste of kombu varies depending on where it was harvested, and each area has its own regulations regarding thickness, width, length, and weight. Here are the four most common varieties.

RAUSU KOMBU

This variety is harvested from the sea around the town of Rausu on the Shiretoko Peninsula, on the east side of Hokkaido. The kombu has rounded edges, so it is easy to distinguish. The stock will be slightly yellow and cloudy, but but it's aromatic and full of umami. I use this often in my cooking.

MA KOMBU

This is harvested in the southwestern part of the Sea of Hokkaido. "Ma" means true or authentic, and as it is called the king of kombu. Stock made with ma-kombu has a pleasant, clean flavor and is likewise transparent. so, this variety is suitable for soups that highlight the color of vegetables.

RISHIRI KOMBU

This type is harvested mostly around the islands of Rishiri and Rebun, in the northernmost part of Hokkaido. Among the four varieties of kombu, I think rishiri kombu makes the most well-rounded and best all-purpose stock. This variety is most often used in high-end restaurants.

HIDAKA KOMBU

A variety harvested in the sea in the southern part of Hokkaido called Hidaka. The fibers of this kombu are very soft, so you can use it not only for stock but also for eating the kombu itself. Though the stock may be a bit cloudy, it has a great flavor and is favored in the Kanto area.

1

MENUS
FOR
GATHERINGS

Menus For Gatherings

1

SUKIYAKI DINNER

═══ MENU ═══

Sukiyaki with Wagyu

--

Seared Katsuo Sashimi

--

Spinach Salad
with Tofu Sauce

SUKIYAKI WITH WAGYU ▸ Serves 4

One of the most requested dishes in my cooking classes is sukiyaki. It's so comforting with the tender slices of wagyu and sweet soy broth. When my family gets together in the winter season, sukiyaki is often the main course. And everyone always looks forward to my mother's repurposing of the leftovers the next day, chopped and added to omelets or mixed into mashed potatoes.

Toppings:
- 200 g / 7 oz. *konnyaku* noodles
  (optional, also called *shirataki*)
- 4 fresh shiitake mushrooms, stems
  removed and crisscross incisions
  cut on caps
- 1 Japanese long onion (*naganegi*),
  cut into 5-cm / 2-in. long pieces on the
  bias
- 170 g / 6 oz. chrysanthemum
  leaves (*shungiku*), cut into 5-cm / 2-in.
  long pieces
- 700g / 1 ½ lb. Chinese cabbage,
  cut into 5-cm long pieces
- 1 block store-bought grilled tofu
  (*yakidofu*), 400 g / 14 oz.,
  cut into 6 to 8 pieces
- 450 g / 1 lb. thinly sliced beef ribeye
  or top round, preferably wagyu

Sukiyaki broth (*Warishita*):
- 300 ml soy sauce
- 300 ml mirin
- 300 ml dashi
- 120 ml sugar

1 Blanch shirataki in a pot of boiling water for a few minutes, drain, and cut lengthwise into three equal portions.

2 Mix all the sukiyaki broth ingredients in a saucepan and bring to a boil. Once it boils, turn off the heat. For an elegant presentation, transfer the broth to a teapot.

3 Arrange all of the vegetables, tofu, and meat on a serving platter to present at the table. Crack one egg in each serving bowl and beat. Set the sukiyaki pan on a portable gas burner at the table.

4 Pour the broth from the teapot into the sukiyaki pan to 1 cm / 1 ½ in. deep and turn on the heat. With the exception of the beef, add whatever variety and quantity of the ingredients that you like to the pan. Allow the ingredients to cook in the hot broth, and add the sliced beef when they are almost completely cooked. Cook the beef very briefly.

5 To eat, dip each ingredient into the beaten egg, like a sauce. As you eat the sukiyaki, continue to refill the pan with ingredients. The broth will reduce, so add more as needed to keep it 1 cm / 1 ½ deep.

SEARED KATSUO SASHIMI ▸ Serves 4

If you don't have a gas flame in your kitchen, simply sear the salted *katsuo* fillet in a heated frying pan with a little bit of vegetable oil.

One 300 g (10 ½ oz.) fillet of katsuo
  (skipjack or bonito), sashimi quality
Salt

Salad (Mix in advance and keep in cold):
  ⅓ Japanese long onion (*naganegi*),
    minced
  2 *myoga* (flower buds of Japanese
    ginger), cut into thin strips
  5 *shiso* leaves, cut into thin strips
  20 g / ⅔ oz. fresh ginger, minced

Ponzu sauce (Mix in advance):
  3 Tablespoons soy sauce
  1 Tablespoon sugar
  2 Tablespoons fresh lemon juice
  2 Tablespoons rice vinegar

1 Soak the paper towels in ice water.
2 Sprinkle the skin side of the katsuo fillet with salt and thread on skewers. Over a gas flame, sear the skin completely. Sear the other sides briefly, just until they become opaque.
3 Wring out the water from the ice-cold paper towels and wrap the fillets to stop the residual cooking.
4 Slice the fillets into 1-cm / ½-in. thick pieces to make sashimi. Place the salad on a plate and arrange the katsuo sashimi on top. Spoon the sauce over the top just before serving.

SPINACH SALAD WITH TOFU SAUCE ▸ Serves 4

This dish doesn't contain any animal ingredients, yet it is rich and satisfying due to the puréed tofu, white miso, and sesame paste.

200 g / 7 oz. fresh spinach
100 g / 3 ½ oz. *shimeji* mushrooms

Tofu sauce:
  1 block (350 g / 12 oz.) *momen* or
    firm tofu, well-drained
  1 Tablespoon soy sauce
  1 Tablespoon sugar
  1 Tablespoon white sesame paste
  1 teaspoon soy sauce

1 To drain the tofu, wrap it with paper towels and place between two cutting boards. Place a heavy weight (like a stack of bowls) on top and allow to drain for 30 minutes, or until the tofu loses almost half of its height. Alternately, cook the wrapped tofu in a 500 watt microwave for 2 minutes, remove paper towels, and allow to cool.
2 Bring water to a boil in a pan. Blanch the spinach for 20-30 seconds and gently squeeze out the excess water by hand. Cut it into approximately 4 cm / 1 ½ in. long pieces. Blanch the shimeji mushrooms for 10 seconds.
3 Place all of the ingredients for the tofu sauce in a food processor and mix into a smooth paste.
4 Dress the spinach and shimeji mushrooms with the tofu sauce.

Menus For Gatherings

2

IZAKAYA DINNER

═══ **MENU** ═══

Onigiri

--

Chicken Wings
with Sweet Soy Sauce

--

Miso Dengaku

CHICKEN WINGS WITH SWEET SOY SAUCE ▸ Serves 4

These still taste great even when they're cold, making them a favorite potluck recipe among my students.

12 chicken wings,
    about 600 g / 1 lb. 5 oz. in total
Potato starch
Vegetable oil

Sauce:
    2 ½ Tablespoons soy sauce
    2 ½ Tablespoons mirin
    2 ½ Tablespoons sake
    2 Tablespoons sugar

White sesame seeds, toasted
Black sesame seeds, toasted

1 Thinly coat the chicken wings with potato starch. Heat vegetable oil in a frying pan over medium heat and sear both sides of the chicken wings until they are golden brown.

2 Combine all of the sauce ingredients in a pan and heat over medium heat. When the sugar dissolves, add the chicken wings and simmer to reduce and thicken the sauce. Turn the wings to coat with the sauce periodically.

3 Turn off the heat, sprinkle with white and black sesame seeds, and toss to distribute evenly.

ONIGIRI ▸ Makes about 8 small rice balls

All Japanese fondly recall their school lunchboxes, especially those containing *onigiri* rice balls. Here is my version, with an appetizing grilled flavor.

560 g / 1 lb. 4 oz. cooked rice, made from
   360 ml short-grain rice
Salt

Miso topping:
   2 Tablespoons sugar
   4 Tablespoons miso
   4 Tablespoons mirin

Roasted sesame oil
4 shiso leaves

Salmon Filling:
   1 salmon fillet, generously salted,
   grilled, then crumbled

1 sheet nori, cut into 8 rectangular pieces

1 For making 4 miso-topped rice balls, wet palms with cold water, sprinkle them with salt, and grab a handful of rice. Shape according to your preference, like balls or triangles. You may also place a piece of plastic wrap on your palm, sprinkle it with salt, and place the rice on top to shape it.

2 Combine all the ingredients for the miso topping.

3 Brush a piece of aluminum foil with the roasted sesame oil and place the rice balls on top. Smear the top of each one with the miso sauce. Broil for several minutes, then turn over and coat the other side with the sauce. Return to the broiler for several additional minutes and broil until the miso topping is slightly charred. Wrap each with a shiso leaf before serving.

4 For making 4 rice balls with salmon filling, mix the crumbled salmon into the rest of the rice. Make rice balls in the same fashion. Cut the nori into pieces for each onigiri, and wrap each just before serving.

MISO DENGAKU ▸ Serves 4

Appetizers or snacks that have been grilled and coated with sweet miso are called miso *dengaku*, and it's a great preparation for vegetables. Feel free to use your favorite style of miso.

Sweet Miso Sauce [Dengaku miso]:
   3 Tablespoons miso
   Haccho-miso was used for the eggplant,
   and white miso for the *nama-fu* in the
   photo.
   1 Tablespoon sake
   2 Tablespoons mirin
   3 Tablespoons sugar

4 Japanese eggplants
2 Tablespoons vegetable oil
4 pieces nama-fu (fresh gluten cake)

1 Place all of the sweet miso sauce ingredients in a small saucepan and turn on the heat. Cook, stirring constantly with a wooden spatula to prevent scorching, until the sauce thickens. It may take several minutes, depending the miso consistency.

2 Remove both ends of the eggplants and cut in half lengthwise. Make several shallow cuts on the flesh side of each eggplant.

3 Heat the vegetable oil in a frying pan, and add eggplants and nama-fu. Cook the eggplants and nama-fu on both sides until they are nicely browned.

4 Place the eggplants and nama-fu on a serving plate. Spoon the sweet miso sauce on top.

Menus For Gatherings

3

VEGETARIAN DINNER

=== MENU ===

Vegetarian Chirashi Sushi

--

Fried Lotus Root Cakes

--

Chawan-mushi

--

Sesami Tofu

VEGETARIAN CHIRASHI SUSHI ▸ Serves 4 to 6

Chirashi sushi is a festive food often enjoyed on Girl's Day in the spring, but it's also popular year-round at gatherings. The seasoned rice can be topped with almost anything, like sashimi, crabmeat, salmon roe, or even made into a vegan preparation.

Seasoned rice, made from 540 ml
   uncooked short-grain rice
   (see p.31 for recipe)

Shiitake and *kampyo*:
   5 dried shiitake mushrooms,
      reconstituted in water
      in the refrigerator for 24 hours
   20 g / ⅔ oz. dried kampyo.
   150 ml shiitake stock*
      *Measure the reconstituting water
      from the shiitakemushrooms, and add
      water if it is less than 150 ml.
   1 ½ Tablespoons sugar
   1 Tablespoon mirin
   1 Tablespoon soy sauce

Lotus Root:
   100 g / 3 ½ oz. lotus root
   2 Tablespoons sugar
   3 Tablespoons rice vinegar
   1 Tablespoon sake

Carrot:
   50 g / 2 oz. carrot
   50 ml dashi
   2 Tablespoons mirin

Omelet:
   3 eggs
   1 teaspoon potato starch
   2 teaspoons sugar
   A pinch salt
   1 Tablespoon vegetable oil

Toppings:
   Mitsuba, toasted white sesame seeds,
   chrysanthemum petals,
   and chopped nori, to taste

1 For prepping the shiitake and kampyo: Remove the hard stems from the shiitake and cut the caps into strips. Reconstitute the kampyo in cold water for 10 minutes, drain, and cut into 1 to 2-cm / ½ -in. pieces. Place the shiitake, kampyo, sugar, mirin, soy sauce, and shiitake stock in a saucepan over medium heat and bring to a simmer. Cook until the liquid nearly evaporates.

2 For prepping the lotus root: Peel the lotus root, cut into quarters lengthwise, and thinly cut each piece crosswise. Combine 1 cup water and 1 teaspoon vinegar [both not written in the ingredient list], and soak the lotus pieces to stop discoloration. Drain the lotus root pieces. Place them in a saucepan and add sugar, rice vinegar, and sake then bring to a simmer. Cook until the liquid nearly evaporates.

3 For prepping the carrot: Cut the carrot into thin strips. Place in a saucepan, add dashi and mirin, and bring to a simmer. Cook until the liquid nearly evaporates.

4 For prepping the eggs: Beat the eggs, add the potato starch, sugar, and salt.
Heat a little of vegetable oil in a frying pan and make 4 to 5 thin omelet sheets. Cut the omelet sheets into 5-cm / 2-in. long thin strips.

5 For assembly: Reserve a little of prepped ingredients for topping. Gently mix the rest of the prepped ingredients into the seasoned rice and arrange onto a serving bowl or platter. Top with the reserved ingredients, mitsuba, toasted white sesame seeds, chrysanthemum petals, and chopped nori.

FRIED LOTUS ROOT CAKES WITH DASHI SAUCE ▸ Serves 4

The dashi sauce really lends a Japanese identity to this dish, but the cakes are also delicious simply sprinkled with salt.

180 g / 6 ½ oz. lotus root
2 Tablespoons flour
1 egg white
A pinch salt
Potato starch
Vegetable oil, for deep frying

Dashi Sauce:
  300 ml dashi
  25 ml mirin
  25 ml soy sauce
  2 teaspoons potato starch, dissolved in 2 teaspoons water in advance
  200 g / 7 oz. daikon radish, grated

Ginger, grated (optional)

1 Peel the lotus root. Weigh out approximately 150 g / 5 oz., and grate it, reserving the liquid as well. Cut the remaining root into 8 mm / ⅓ in. cubes. Mix the grated lotus root, its liquid, cubed lotus root, flour, egg white, and salt in a bowl and mix well. It should be possible to shape it, so if it's too runny add more flour.
2 Heat the oil to 160°C / 320°F.
3 Shape the lotus root mixture into rounds, thinly coat with the potato starch, and deep fry for 5 to 10 minutes until golden brown.
4 For making the dashi sauce: Combine the dashi with the mirin and soy sauce in a saucepan and bring to a simmer. Add the potato starch and grated daikon, simmer for several minutes, and turn off the heat.
5 Arrange the fried lotus root cakes in individual dishes and spoon the sauce over the top.

CHAWAN-MUSHI ▸ Serves 4

Though it looks like pudding, it's not sweet. This savory custard showcases the flavor of the dashi, and hidden internal garnishes add excitement to the texture.

200 g / 7oz. *kinu* tofu,
    silken tofu or soft tofu
2 shiitake mushrooms
2 eggs
300 ml dashi
½ Tablespoon soy sauce
A pinch salt

Mitsuba leaves (or sprigs of chervil)

1 Wrap the lid of a steamer with a cloth to prevent the water from dripping into the custards. Add water and turn on the heat in preparation for steaming.
2 Cut the tofu into 4 pieces. Slice the mushrooms into thin pieces. Set aside.
3 Beat the eggs in a mixing bowl, and add the dashi, soy sauce, and salt. Strain through a fine mesh sieve to get rid of any lumps of eggs.
4 Place a piece of tofu and a few slices of mushrooms in each cup. Slowly pour in the egg mixture. Top each with the mitsuba leaves.
5 Place the cups in the steamer. Place chopsticks between the steamer pot and the lid to keep the inside of the pan at a constant temperature of approximately 80°C / 176°F. Steam over high heat for 3 minutes. Reduce the heat and continue to steam over low heat for 10 minutes or until set.

SESAME TOFU

▸ Makes 1 block from a stainless-steel mold,
  15 cm / 6 in. square

It often comes in a block, so it is often referred to as tofu though it's not. It's a Zen temple vegetarian dish that showcases the nutty flavor of sesame seeds. Unsalted peanut butter may be substituted for the sesame paste.

70 g / 2 ½ oz. *kudzu* starch
4 Tablespoons black sesame paste
    (or white sesame paste)
600 ml kombu dashi (see p.10 for recipe)
A pinch salt
Wasabi paste, to taste
Soy sauce, to taste

1 First dissolve the kudzu starch with a little of the kombu dashi in a bowl. Next add the rest of kombu dashi, sesame paste, and salt. Mix well.
2 Strain the mixture into a saucepan. Cook over medium heat, stirring constantly with a wooden spatula to prevent scorching. When the mixture thickens to a mashed potato-like consistency, continue stirring for another 15 minutes.
3 Wipe the mold with a wet towel and pour the mixture in it. Let it cool in ice water. Place the ice water on top of the mixture to prevent it from drying out (you can pour ice water on it directly.)
4 When the mixture has set, cut into squares.
5 Arrange in individual bowls. Serve with wasabi paste and soy sauce.

The Japanese style of everyday at-home dining almost always includes a bowl of cooked short-grain rice, a bowl of soup, and several other small dishes served alongside as accompaniments. We often make two or three small dishes using seasonal ingredients, and we consider one of the dishes, like sautéed meat or grilled dish, as the main course. The others, like salad or pickled vegetables, are side dishes. This style of eating naturally provides a balanced and nutritious set meal, called *ichiju-sansai* (one bowl of soup and three dishes) or *ichiju-nisai* (one bowl of soup and two dishes). We've grown up hearing these words from our grandmothers and mothers often repeated like a mantra.

The bowl of soup is usually miso soup, made grilled or simmered in flavorful, seasoned dashi. For the side dishes, I like to use seasonal vegetables, many varieties of beans, and seaweeds. If you grill fish for the main course, choose another cooking method for the vegetable side dishes to provide contrast. Choosing a variety of cooking methods and seasonings in the menu is one of the foundations of Japanese cooking.

So when you build a meal set, simply try to include variety which will create a balance in nutrition, flavor, and eye appeal. Grilling, boiling, simmering, deep-frying, and raw preparations are common. Sweet soy sauce (*ama-kara*), acidity, pure soy sauce, miso, and fresh components are often-used seasonings.

HOW TO BUILD A JAPANESE MEAL SET

from dashi and one's own favorite type of miso. My students are surprised when I tell them that I often eat miso soup three times per day. But the variations of miso soup are innumerable—eggplant in the summer, mushroom and squash in the fall, and hearty root vegetables in the winter. I love to combine seasonal ingredients with tofu cubes for endless variety; you can explore your own favorite combinations of ingredients. My mother is from Hokkaido, and believe me, their miso soup with Hokkaido potatoes and milk is absolutely fantastic. My husband's mother makes her version of miso soup with beaten eggs, which I'd never even heard of before I married him.

For the main dish, I love to serve fish either

In Japanese cooking, many dishes are seasoned with ama-kara. If I've chosen a main course seasoned this way, I make sure to choose contrasting side dishes. If the main course is deep-fried, a selection of vegetables seasoned with vinegar would be a good choice.

Also, we don't make every dish on the same day it is served, and side dishes don't have to be complicated. I simmer and season the beans or vegetables a day ahead and keep them in the refrigerator, as in the case of Spinach Salad with Sweet Sesame Sauce. When tomatoes are ripe and especially flavorful in the summer, I simply slice them and consider that as one of the side dishes.

2

DISHES
WITH
UNIVERSAL
APPEAL

THICK
SUSHI
ROLLS
[FUTOMAKI]

My students are often surprised when I tell them that I only go to eat sushi in a restaurant once per year. I would guess that sushi connoisseurs overseas eat sushi more often than most Japanese people! But for festive family occasions and for my husband's lunch box, I often make sushi rolls. When preparing this for a bento box, omit the sashimi.

THICK SUSHI ROLLS [FUTOMAKI] ▸ Makes 6 thick rolls

6 sheets of nori, each approximately
  21 × 19 cm / 8 in. square
Seasoned rice, made from 540 ml
  uncooked short-grain rice
  (See below for recipe)
Te-zu (½ cup water combined
  with 2 teaspoons vinegar)
  *Te-zu is used to prevent the rice from
  sticking to the hands.

Toppings:
  Wasabi paste (optional)
  Japanese cucumber, halved lengthwise
    and cut into 4 to 6 pieces lengthwise

  Shiso leaves
  Sashmi, such as tuna or salmon
  Avocado
  Egg omelet sheets (*Tamago-yaki*)
  Boiled shrimp

1 Place a bamboo mat flat side up. Position a sheet of nori with the shiny side down and the longer side facing to you.
2 Moisten both hands with te-zu, and grab about 250 g / 8 to 9 oz. of rice. Thinly spread the rice over the nori, leaving a 3 to 4-cm / 1 ½ - inch strip on the side opposite of you for sealing the nori.
3 Create a channel in the center of the rice with your fingers along the length of the nori. Thinly smear some wasabi paste along the channel, if using. Lay a thin layer of chosen toppings on top.
4 Using both hands, begin rolling by holding the bamboo mat and nori at the same time with the thumbs and index fingers, and holding the toppings intact with the other fingers. Continue to roll gently without too much pressure, pressing the mat delicately to make a fluffy, round log.
5 Remove the bamboo mat once and make sure the seam is on the underside. Cover the log with the bamboo mat again and reshape into a neater round log. Repeat the same process with the other sheets of nori.
6 Cut each log equally into 8 round pieces.

SEASONED RICE ▸ Makes about 1,050 g / 37 ½ oz.

540 ml short-grain rice
500 ml water

Rice seasoning:
  6 Tablespoons rice vinegar
  5 Tablespoons sugar
  1 teaspoon salt

1 Wash the rice with cold water several times and cook in the water.
2 Meanwhile, combine all of the rice seasoning ingredients in a glass bowl. If the sugar doesn't dissolve completely, microwave it until it dissolves. Do not let it boil or the tartness of the vinegar will dissipate.
3 Soak a wooden tub until it has absorbed some water, then dry with a paper towel. Alternately, you may use a large bowl.
4 Place the freshly-cooked rice into the wooden tub, then slowly and indirectly add the rice seasoning by pouring it onto a wooden spatula. By holding the spatula flat side up, distribute the rice seasoning into the rice by moving the spatula in a cutting motion from side to side. Do not mix vigorously or the rice will become sticky.
5 Cool the top layer of rice by fanning it, then gently fold the rice from the bottom to the surface and cool it by fanning again. Cover with a damp cloth to prevent it from drying, and set aside until the rice reaches body temperature before making sushi. (The rice will become too hard to make sushi if it is refrigerated.)

NON-FRIED NANBAN-ZUKE WITH SALMON FILLETS ▸ Serves 4

Nanban-zuke is a sweet-piquant dish of marinated seafood and vegetables. It's not particularly tart, but rather savory and thus makes a great appetizer-sized portion or sandwich filling. Fish and meat are often deep fried, but here is a pan-fried version which uses less oil.

2 onions, thinly sliced
1 carrot, cut into thin strips
3 bell peppers, cut into thin strips

Marinade:
    135 ml rice vinegar
    135 ml sake
    135 ml mirin
    90 ml soy sauce
    1 to 2 dried hot chili peppers, seeded

4 slices fresh salmon, each 70 g / 2 ½ oz.
2 teaspoons vegetable oil
Potato starch (or cornstarch)

1 Mix all the marinade ingredients in a saucepan, bring to a boil, and immediately turn off the heat. Transfer the marinade to a shallow pan and add the onions, carrot, and bell peppers.

2 Cut each salmon slice into 4 to 5 pieces and remove any pin bones.

3 Heat the vegetable oil in a frying pan. Thinly coat the salmon with potato starch and cook until both sides become golden brown and the flesh is just cooked through. Transfer the salmon to the marinade while hot, and allow to marinate in the refrigerator. You can eat them after marinating for an hour, but they are also great after 2 days of marinating.

NANBAN-ZUKE WITH CHICKEN THIGHS ▸ Serves 4

In Japan, *nanban-zuke* made with chicken is as popular as it is with seafood. The sweet and sour marinade goes well with the fried chicken, and it's irresistible with the homemade tartar sauce. If you want to be authentic, use Japanese mayonnaise (such as Kewpie). Many of my students have fallen in love with its addictive taste.

550 g / 1 lb. 3 oz. chicken thighs,
    cut into large bite-sized pieces
Salt
Flour
1 egg, beaten
Vegetable oil for deep frying

Marinade:
    3 Tablespoons soy sauce
    2 Tablespoons sugar
    5 Tablespoons rice vinegar
    1 Tablespoon mirin
    1 to 2 dried hot chili peppers,
       seeded

Tartar sauce:
    2 boiled eggs, roughly mashed
       with a fork
    ¼ onion, chopped
    4 Tablespoons mayonnaise
    1 Tablespoon tomato ketchup
    1 teaspoon fresh lemon juice
    1 teaspoon rice vinegar
    A pinch salt

Shredded cabbage
Shredded shiso leaves

1 Season the chicken thighs with the salt. Thinly coat with the flour, dredge well in the egg, and deep fry at 170°C / 340°F until golden brown.
2 Meanwhile combine all of the marinade ingredients in a shallow pan and add the chicken thighs as they finish frying to marinate.
3 Mix all the tartar sauce ingredients in a bowl.
4 Mix the cabbage and shiso leaves and arrange on a plate along with the marinated chicken thighs. Spoon the tartar sauce over the chicken.

CREAMY CRABMEAT CROQUETS ▸ Serves 4

Enjoy the creaminess of béchamel with the rich umami from crabmeat and tonkatsu sauce (a Japanese version of Worcestershire sauce). I've increased the flour to make the croquets easy-to-shape, but you may decrease the flour to 60 g / 2 oz. for a more unctuous texture.

1 onion, finely chopped
1 Tablespoons vegetable oil
1 can of crabmeat, about 150 g / 3 ½ oz.
A pinch salt

Béchamel sauce:
    70 g / 2 ½ oz. butter
    80 g / 3 oz. flour
    600 ml whole milk, room temperature

Salt
Flour
2 eggs, beaten
About 200 ml panko
    (Japanese bread crumbs)
Vegetable oil for deep frying

Tonkatsu sauce
Shredded cabbage

1 Place vegetable oil and onion in a frying pan and cook until the onion is softened. Add the crabmeat and cook for a few additional minutes.

2 For the béchamel sauce: Melt the butter in a frying pan over low heat. Stir in the flour and mix until smooth. Add the milk in small batches, whisking with each addition until it is completely incorporated.

3 Add the onion and crabmeat mixture to the béchamel sauce. Season the mixture with the salt to taste. Spread evenly on a sheet tray, cover, and chill in the refrigerator for several hours.

4 Divide the mixture into 12 pieces. Thinly coat your palms with vegetable oil and shape each piece into a cylinder.

5 Coat each with flour, then egg, and finally panko. Deep fry in 170°C / 340°F oil. Drain on a wire rack.

6 Arrange the croquets and shredded cabbage on individual plates. Serve with tonkatsu sauce.

SESAME DRESSING ▸ Serves 4

Japanese use sesame dressing often on their salads, so there are many commercially-produced varieties available in the supermarket. But nothing beats homemade sesame dressing, with its fresh, nutty aroma. Simply spoon it over fresh salad greens, or steamed, roasted or grilled vegetables.

Your favorite vegetables, cooked as desired
  (Steamed broccoli, sweet potato, and kabocha squash are shown in the photo.)

Sesame Dressing:
  5 Tablespoons white sesame paste
  3 Tablespoons rice vinegar
  2 Tablespoons sugar
  1 Tablespoon soy sauce
  1 Tablespoon mirin
  1 Tablespoon vegetable oil

Combine the dressing ingredients and mix well. The consistency can be adjusted to your liking by adding 1 to 3 tablespoons of dashi. Arrange vegetables on a serving platter and spoon the sauce over the top.

SALT-CURED SALMON SOUP [SANPEI-JIRU] ▸ Serves 4

This is a local dish popular in my mother's hometown in Hokkaido, the northernmost prefecture known for its frigid winters. It's a simple dish made by stewing salt-cured salmon with root vegetables, but the comforting salty-sweet flavor always wins over my students.

200 g / 7 oz. store-bought skin-on
  salted salmon (*shio-zake*)
1 L kombu dashi
10-cm / 4-in. long piece of daikon radish,
  cut into thin rounds and quartered
½ carrot, cut like the daikon
1 potato, cut into 2-cm / 1-in. cubes
2 Tablespoons sake
A pinch salt
1 green onion, finely chopped

1 Cut the salmon into bite-sized pieces.
2 Heat the kombu dashi over medium high heat. Add the daikon, carrot, and potato. When the vegetables are almost cooked, add the salmon pieces and cook for 15 minutes.
3 Season with the sake and salt. Lastly add the green onion. Remove from the heat and serve in individual bowls.

SUSHI POCKETS [INARI-ZUSHI]

▸ Makes 8 pieces

My vegetarian students have said that inari-zushi is one of their favorite bento box lunches. Any kind of dashi can be used to simmer and season the *abura-age* (fried tofu pouches), but I recommend shiitake dashi since the mushroom flavor really complements the sweet soy sauce. To enjoy a variation, I often mix sesame seeds into the seasoned rice.

4 sheets abura-age (fried tofu pouches)

Simmering liquid:
   1 ½ Tablespoons sugar
   1 ½ Tablespoons soy sauce
   1 ½ Tablespoons mirin
   300 ml shiitake dashi (see p.10 for recipe)

Seasoned rice, made from 180 ml
   uncooked short-grain rice
   (see p.31 for recipe)

1 Cut each abura-age in half and open each pouch by hand. If it's hard to open, place it on a cutting board and roll with a rolling pin.

2 Bring water to a boil in a medium sauce pan, blanch the abura-age for few seconds to remove some of the oil, shock in cold water, and drain.

3 Combine all of the seasoned rice ingredients in a sauce pan, put a drop-lid on top (it will keep the abura age flat during cooking), cover with a regular lid, and cook for approximately 20 minutes. If liquid still remains, remove both lids and reduce until it is nearly gone.

4 Stuff each abura-age piece about ³/₄ full with the seasoned rice, then fold the edge to close the pocket.

MASHED POTATO CAKES
[IMO-MOCHI]

▸ Makes 4 patties

One of my students learned how to make these Japanese-style mashed potato cakes in class, and now he makes them every year for Christmas back home in Germany. For an easy variation, I wrap a piece of cheese in the mashed potato or I substitute sweet potatoes for the potatoes. Either way, enjoy the cakes while piping hot.

2 medium sized potatoes,
　　about 200 g / 7 oz. in total
5 Tablespoons potato starch
1 Tablespoon vegetable oil

Teriyaki sauce (Mix in advance):
　　4 Tablespoons sugar
　　2 Tablespoons soy sauce
　　2 Tablespoons sake

1 Peel the potatoes and cut into chunks. Bring water to a boil in a large pot. Reduce the heat to medium-low and simmer the potatoes until tender, about 15 to 20 minutes. Drain the potatoes and immediately return them to the pan. Cook over medium heat to evaporate the water and make the surface of the potatoes fluffy.

2 Mash the potatoes while hot until smooth, and mix well with the potato starch to develop some tackiness. Shape into four patties.

3 Place vegetable oil in a frying pan and cook the patties on both sides until lightly golden. Add the teriyaki sauce and reduce, flipping the patties, until the sauce has thickened.

VEGETARIAN PUDDING WITH BLACK SESAME SEEDS

▶ Serves 4

I prefer to use *kudzu* starch instead of animal gelatin because it gives puddings a smoother texture. The main ingredient in this recipe is soy milk, and it's vegetarian, gluten and dairy-free.

300 ml soy milk
2 Tablespoons kudzu starch
2 Tablespoons black sesame paste
4 Tablespoons granulated sugar

1 Combine 2 tablespoons of soy milk with the kudzu starch in a bowl, dissolving the starch completely. Add the black sesame paste and sugar. Add the remaining soy milk gradually, completely dissolving the sugar.

2 Strain the mixture through a fine mesh sieve into a medium saucepan.

3 Bring the mixture to a simmer over low heat, stirring constantly with a wooden spatula. Continue to cook as the mixture thickens, stirring, for 5 minutes.

4 Pour the mixture into cups and let set in the refrigerator.

TOFU "CREAM" CAKE

▸ Makes one round cake 18 cm / 7 inches in diameter

Many students ask how to use tofu other than in salads or as an appetizer, and I always teach them this recipe. Well-drained tofu lends creaminess, smoothness and richness to this surprisingly satisfying cake. It's even better the next day when it's even more moist.

Crust:

    25 g rapeseed oil

    35 g maple syrup

    80 g cake flour, sifted

Tofu Cream:

    2 blocks *momen* or firm tofu,

        700 g / 1 ½ lb. in total, well-drained

        *See p.17 for draining procedure.

    10 g *kudzu* powder

    40 g almond powder

    120 g rice syrup

    50 g maple syrup

    50 g rapeseed oil

    3 Tablespoons juiced lemon

Few drops vanilla extract

1 For the crust: Combine the rapeseed oil with the maple syrup, add the flour, and lightly mix with a rubber spatula. Do not over mix. Press the crust mixture into the bottom and sides of the mold. Poke with a fork and bake in a 170°C/ 340F oven for 15 minutes.

2 For the tofu cream: Purée the drained tofu in a food processor until smooth, add the remaining ingredients of the tofu cream, and purée until smooth.

3 Spread the tofu cream over the baked crust while still in the mold, then bake in a 170°C / 340°F oven for 50 minutes, until the top is nicely browned.

4 Let it cool on a wire rack in the mold. Unmold and cut into wedges.

3

FISH
&
SEAFOOD

MISO-SIMMERED MACKEREL ▸ Serves 4

One of the advantages in my cooking classes is that we have access to the freshest fish from Tsukiji. If your fish has a slight fishy smell, I recommend pouring boiling water over it and then rinsing with ice water. A generous amount of ginger also helps to mask the fishiness.

Miso broth:
    4 ½ Tablespoons red miso
    4 ½ Tablespoons sugar
    4 ½ Tablespoons mirin
    4 ½ Tablespoons sake
    1 ½ Tablespoons soy sauce
    150 ml water

4 slices of mackerel, about 100 g / 3 ½ oz. each
15-g / ½-oz. piece of ginger, sliced

Place all of the ingredients for the miso broth in a pan and cook over medium
heat until warm. Add the sliced mackerel and sliced ginger, cover with a
drop-lid, and simmer for about 10 to 15 minutes, basting the mackerel with the
miso broth occasionally to create sheen. Don't flip the mackerel over during
cooking or it will break apart.

SAKE-STEAMED CLAMS

One day I received a request from a student to learn how to make steamed clams with sake, which she first saw on a popular TV show in Asia called *Shinya Shokudo* ("Midnight Diner"), which is based on a manga comic series. When you open the lid of the pan, the sweet aromas of sake and butter waft up and stimulate your appetite.

SWORDFISH TERIYAKI

Many people love swordfish, kajiki, because it's meaty and re-
sembles chicken. It also goes great with teriyaki sauce. Over-
cooking it will result in a tough and dry texture, just like over-
cooked chicken, so be attentive to the cooking time. My teriyaki
sauce recipe is very versatile, and you can use it for almost anything including chicken, beef, or salmon.

CHOPPED SASHIMI [NAMEROU] & ITS TEMPURA

One day I received a request from a student to learn how to make steamed clams with sake. She first saw the recipe on the food drama called Shinya Shoduo (Midnight Diner), which is based on a manga comic series. When you open the lid of the pan, the sweet aromas of sake and butter waft up and stimulate your appetite.

RICE BOWL WITH TEMPURA [TEN-DON]

When deep-frying at home with a limited amount of oil, omitting eggs will result in a much lighter and crispier tempura. The keys for success are simple: chill the flour and water in the refrigerator, don't over-mix the batter, and try to maintain the oil temperature. You can eat this tempura on its own, but it's also great served atop rice for a satisfying lunch.

SAKE-STEAMED CLAMS ▸ Serves 4

500 g / 1 lb. 2 oz. live *asari* clams
    (or littleneck or steamer clams)
1 clove garlic, sliced
1 teaspoon vegetable oil
200 ml sake
1 ½ tablespoons butter
2 teaspoons soy sauce
½ Japanese long onion (*naganegi*),
    chopped

1 Soak the clams in salted water (mix 1 tablespoon salt with 500 ml water), cover to block any light, and allow to sit in a cool place for 20 minutes while the clams expel sand.

2 Place the sliced garlic and vegetable oil in a frying pan over medium heat and fry the garlic until fragrant. Add the clams and sake, increase the heat to high, and cover with a lid to steam the clams and let the shells open up.

3 Discard any unopened clams. Add butter, soy sauce, and chopped green onions, stir, and turn off the heat.

4 Arrange the clams in a shallow bowl with their broth.

SWORDFISH TERIYAKI ▸ Serves 4

4 pieces of swordfish,
    about 120 g / 4 ½ oz. each
1 teaspoon salt
1 teaspoon vegetable oil

Teriyaki sauce (Mix in advance):
    1 ½ Tablespoons sake
    2 Tablespoons mirin
    2 Tablespoons soy sauce
    1 Tablespoon sugar

1 Sprinkle each piece of swordfish with salt, let it sit for 5 minutes, and wipe off any excess water from the surface.

2 Warm the vegetable oil in a frying pan, add the swordfish, and lightly cook both sides for 4 to 6 minutes in total.

3 Add the teriyaki sauce and cook the swordfish, basting from time to time, until the sauce thickens to a syrupy consistency.

CHOPPED SASHIMI [NAMEROU] & ITS TEMPURA ▸ 8 Peaces

1 fresh whole *aji*, about 200 g / 7 oz.
2 Tablespoons chopped green onions
2 teaspoons chopped ginger
1 Tablespoon yellow miso

For the tempura:
    8 fresh shiitake mushrooms,
      stems removed
    5 Tablespoons flour
    4 Tablespoons water
    Vegetable oil

For making namerou, cut the aji into two fillets, remove the bones and skin, and roughly chop the fillets into small pieces. Using a knife, chop them along with the green onions, ginger and miso until the mixture becomes almost a paste. This can be served as-is at this point and pairs well with sake or with cooked rice.

For making tempura, stuff the shiitake with the namerou. Mix the flour and water in a bowl, coat the stuffed shiitake with the batter, and deep fry in 170°C / 340°F oil until the batter becomes crisp and golden brown.

RICE BOWL WITH TEMPURA [TEN-DON]

▶ Serves 4

Tempura sauce (*Tentsuyu*):
  ¼ cup soy sauce
  ¼ cup mirin
  1 Tablespoon sugar
  ½ cup dashi

1 cup flour, chilled in the refrigerator
1 cup water, chilled in the
    refrigerator
A medium bowl for mixing the batter,
    chilled in the refrigerator
Vegetable oil
8 fresh shiitake mushrooms,
    stems removed
About ¼ *kabocha* squash
8 large shrimp

Kakiage tempura:
  ½ onion, sliced
  ¼ carrot, cut into thin strips
  4 Tablespoons dried shrimp
    (*sakura-ebi*)
  1 Tablespoon flour

4 servings of cooked rice

1 For the tempura sauce: bring all of the ingredients to a boil in a saucepan then remove from the heat. Allow to cool at room temperature.

2 Remove the stems from the shiitake mushrooms. Remove the seeds from the squash and cut into 8-mm / ⅓ -in thick wedges (you will need 8 slices). Cut the onion into thin slices. Peel the shrimp, devein, and make a few shallow cuts on the belly side of each one to prevent them from curling during cooking. Dry with paper towels.

3 Place the chilled flour and water in the chilled bowl and mix with chopsticks a few times. Do not over-mix or the batter will become sticky and heavy. Place the batter in the refrigerator until ready to use.

4 Heat the oil to 170°C / 340°F.

5 For frying the shitake and squash: dip them in batter to coat lightly, and deep-fry until golden brown. As it fries, dip in the tempura sauce and drain on a tray lined with a wire rack.

6 For frying the kakiage: combine the onion, carrot, and dried shrimp with the flour in a bowl. Add about 7 tablespoon of the remaining batter and mix until the ingredients barely hold together. Place one quarter of the mixture on a large wooden spatula and slip it into 170°C /340°F oil. Repeat with the remaining batter. As each piece finishes frying, dip in the tempura sauce and drain as well.

7 For frying the shrimp: lightly coat the shrimp with flour, dip in the batter, and fry in 180°C / 360°F oil. Dip in the tempura sauce and drain as well.

8 Spoon some of the rice into individual serving bowls, top variety of tempura, and spoon some of the tempura sauce on top to taste.

4

MEAT

&

POULTRY

CHICKEN TERIYAKI ▸ Serves 4

Once you begin to make your own teriyaki sauce, your teriyaki repertoire will really expand. We will start with the teriyaki sauce we made for the Swordfish Teriyaki (see p. 45) but I'll add a bit more sugar and some honey to make it sweeter to pair with the chicken.

2 chicken thighs, about 500 g
   / 1 lb. 2 oz. in total
4 pinches salt
2 Tablespoons sake

Teriyaki sauce (Mix in advance):
   2 Tablespoons soy sauce
   2 Tablespoons mirin
   1 ½ Tablespoons sugar
   1 ½ Tablespoons sake
   1 ½ Tablespoons honey

1 Japanese long onion (*naganegi*)

1 Cut each chicken thigh in half, trim off any excess fat and poke holes with a fork on the skin side. Rub each half with a pinch of salt and ½ tablespoon of sake and let it sit for 10 minutes.

2 Cut the long onion into 4-cm / 1 ½-in. long pieces, and make thin slits on the surface of each one.

3 Use a non-stick frying pan. Place the chicken skin-side down along with the long onion pieces in the pan over medium heat. When the chicken skins becomes nicely golden brown, flip, and cook the other side. Flip the long onion occasionally and cook evenly.

4 Remove the long onion from the pan, wipe out any residual fat or liquid with paper towels and add the teriyaki sauce to the pan. Cook the chicken until the sauce thickens, basting occasionally.

5 Return the long onion to the pan, toss with the sauce, then arrange the chicken, long onion, and the sauce on a plate.

JAPANESE-STYLE FRIED CHICKEN
[KARA-AGE]

Japanese fried chicken is extra-crispy because it is fried with potato starch (or cornstarch). The coating won't absorb as much
oil, so it's healthier than regular fried chick-
en. This recipe makes enough for a snack
for four people, but it can be increased to
make enough for dinner along with rice and
grated daikon radish.

RICE BOWL WITH PORK TONKATSU
[KATSUDON]

Living in the United States, some of my American friends told me how much they loved katsudon and how they would venture to Japanese restaurants weekly to get their fix. They craved the unique combination of the fried pork with the flavorful stock. When preparing this dish, I ask how each person prefers their eggs cooked since some people don't care for runny eggs.

BRAISED PORK BELLY

Some recipes indicate that the pork belly should be boiled, but I recommend steaming it instead for an unctuous and very tender texture. Steaming the pork belly for over an hour with long onion, ginger, and sake will eliminate any strong pork odor. You may have some flavorful juices from the pork during steaming. I often mix the juices with mashed potatoes and serve them with the braised pork belly on top.

JAPANESE-STYLE POT STICKERS
[GYOZA]

These are a hybrid of Chinese pot stickers, but even Chinese students want to learn how to make these flavorful dumplings. Since many people want to increase their vegetable consumption, more vegetables than pork are used in this recipe. If you prefer a completely vegetarian version, you can replace the meat with chopped fresh shiitake mushrooms or *okara* (soy pulp filtered from soy milk during tofu production).

JAPANESE-STYLE FRIED CHICKEN
[KARA-AGE] ▶ Serves 4 as a beer snack

Marinade (Mix in advance):
  3 Tablespoons soy sauce
  4 Tablespoons sake
  2 pieces ground ginger
  2 pieces ground garlic

2 chicken thighs, about 500 g
  / 1 lb. 2 oz. in total
Potato starch (or cornstarch)
Vegetable oil
Salt and pepper, as needed

1 Cut the chicken into bite-sized pieces, combine with the marinade in a sealed plastic bag, and allow to marinate in the refrigerator for at least 30 minutes. If you prefer a richer taste you can marinate overnight.
2 Drain the chicken, lightly pat dry, and coat with the potato starch.
3 Working in small batches, deep-fry the chicken pieces in the 170 to 180°C / 340 to 360°F oil until the surface becomes golden brown.
4 Arrange onto a plate sprinkled with a mixture of salt and pepper.

RICE BOWL
WITH PORK TONKATSU [KATSUDON] ▶ Serves 4

Panko-fried pork (Tonkatsu):
  4 slices center-cut pork loin,
    each 1 cm / approximately ½
    in. thick and 120 g / 4 ½ oz.
  4 pinches salt
  1 cup panko (Japanese bread
  crumbs)
  1 egg, beaten
  Flour, for dredging
  Vegetable oil for pan-frying

8 eggs
2 onions

Cooking sauce:
  200 ml dashi
  4 Tablespoons soy sauce
  4 Tablespoons mirin
  4 Tablespoons sake
  4 Tablespoons sugar

4 servings cooked short-grain rice
1 heaping Tablespoon chopped
  green onion

1 Make slashes on both sides of the pork slices to keep the meat from curling when frying. Rub with salt. Dredge each in flour, then beaten egg and finally panko. Deep fry the pork slices in a frying pan with about 1.25 cm / 1 in. deep oil until golden brown. Drain and then slice each piece into 5 to 6 strips. Set aside.
2 Roughly beat the eggs, set aside.
3 Thinly slice the onions and combine them with the cooking sauce ingredients in a large sauce pan (about 26 cm / 10 ½ in. in diameter). Cook over medium heat until the onions become tender, approximately 5 to 10 minutes.
4 Cook two servings in the first batch: Remove half of the onions and half of the cooking liquid and set aside. Place half of the panko-fried pork pieces on top of the remaining onions and cooking liquid (in the pan) and pour one quarter of the beaten eggs. Cover and simmer the panko-fried pork undisturbed over low heat for 5 to 6 minutes. Pour another quarter of the beaten eggs, cover, and simmer undisturbed for 30 seconds.
5 Repeat [step 4] with the rest of the onions with cooking liquids, tonkatsu, and beaten eggs to make another two-servings.
6 Portion warm rice into large individual serving bowls, top with the tonkatsu-egg mixture and some of the cooking sauce from the pan . Garnish with chopped green onions.

BRAISED PORK BELLY ▸ Serves 4

A block of fresh pork belly or
    shoulder, about 600 g / 1 lb. 5 oz.
½ Japanese long onion (*naganegi*)
    or 2 green onions
20 g / ⅔ oz. ginger
60 ml sake

Simmering liquid:
    400 ml water
    80 ml soy sauce
    60 ml sake
    4 tablespoons sugar

4 hard-boiled eggs, peeled
Japanese mustard, to taste

1 Cut the long onion into 3-cm / 1-in. long pieces.
Thinly slice the ginger.
2 Place the block of pork belly on a tray or shallow
dish that holds liquid, and cover with the long onion
pieces and sliced ginger. Sprinkle with the sake. Place
the tray in a steamer and steam for at least an hour and
a half.
3 Transfer the pork belly to another tray or dish and
let it cool in the refrigerator for several hours.
4 Cut the pork belly into bite-sized pieces. Place them
in a saucepan along with the simmering liquid and
boiled eggs, and bring it to a simmer.
5 Arrange in a bowl along with the reduced sauce.
Serve with the mustard.

JAPANESE-STYLE POT STICKERS [GYOZA] ▸ Serves 4

Filling:
    150 g / 5 ½ oz. ground pork
    2 leaves of cabbage, minced
    100 g / 3 ½ oz. Chinese chives,
        minced
    ½ green onion, minced
    20 g / ⅔ oz. ginger, grated
    1 clove garlic, grated
    ½ Tablespoon oyster sauce
    1 Tablespoon sake
    1 Tablespoon soy sauce
    ½ Tablespoon sesame oil

1 pack gyoza wrappers
    (or pot sticker wrappers),
    about 25 sheets
1 Tablespoon vegetable oil

Dipping sauce (Mix in advance):
    3 Tablespoons soy sauce
    1 Tablespoon rice vinegar
    Chinese chili oil (la-yu)

1 Place all of the filling ingredients in a bowl and
knead well by hand until somewhat sticky. Let it sit
for 5 minutes.
2 Place one wrapper in your palm and spread approximately a tablespoon of the filling in the center. Smear
water along the edge of the circle with your finger.
Fold in half with the filling in the middle, pinch the
edges of the semi-circle at several places to make pleats
and create a seal.
3 Place the oil and dumplings, sealed-side up, in a
single layer in a frying pan, preferably non-stick, over
medium-high heat and cook them until the bottoms are
golden-brown.
4 Add about ¼ cup of water along the edge of the pan
and cover. Let the dumplings steam until the water is
gone, for approximately 5 minutes.
5 Uncover and arrange the dumplings on a serving
plate. Pour the dipping sauce into a small dish and
serve alongside.

5

VEGETABLES

&

TOFU

SPINACH SALAD
WITH SWEET SESAME SAUCE ▸ Serves 4

When you want to serve vegetables, but not necessarily a raw salad, try this dish. Greens are blanched and tossed with sweet sesame sauce, and it becomes an incredibly versatile dish. It can be served with hot cooked rice, as an appetizer, or as an accompaniment to sake or beer. The dressing is also great with other kinds of vegetables, and the easy ratio is 4 parts sesame seeds to one part each soy sauce and sugar.

200 g / 7 oz. fresh spinach

Sweet sesame sauce:
   2 Tablespoons white sesame seeds,
     toasted and ground
   1/2 Tablespoon soy sauce
   1/2 Tablespoon sugar

1 Blanch the spinach in the boiling water for about 30 seconds, shock in ice water, lightly squeeze out excess water by hand, and cut into 3 to 4-cm / 1 1/2- in. long pieces.
2 Combine the dressing ingredients in a bowl, add the spinach, and toss well with chopsticks.

TUNA AND GREEN ONIONS
WITH SWEET-SOUR MISO SAUCE ▸ Serves 4

This classic appetizer goes well with cold sake, and is often served in Japanese homes and upscale izakayas. The sauce gets a bit of a kick from Japanese mustard that accents the sweet-sour flavors. It will keep for several days in the refrigerator and can be used as a dressing for sashimi or grilled items like mushrooms or squid.

200 g / 7 oz. sashimi-quality tuna
   (or any seafood such as fresh
   squid or octopus)
160 g / 6 oz. green onions
A pinch salt
1 Tablespoon rice vinegar

Sweet-sour miso sauce :
   1 Tablespoon sake
   1 1/2 Tablespoons sugar
   2 Tablespoons white miso
     (or any type of miso)
   1 Tablespoon rice vinegar
   1 teaspoon Japanese mustard paste

1 Cut the white and light green parts from the soft dark green tops of the onions. Blanch the white and light green parts first for 30 seconds then add the dark green tops and cook for 10 additional seconds. Drain, and fan them out to allow them to cool. Using the back of a knife, scrape out the gel-like substance from the inside of the onion. Cut each into 3 to 4-cm / 1 1/2-in. long pieces.
2 Cut the tuna into 1 cm / 1/2 in. dice.
3 Combine the sauce ingredients in a small sauce pan, bring to a simmer over medium heat, and cook for 1 to 2 minutes. Remove from the heat and add the mustard paste.
4 Arrange the green onions and diced tuna in individual serving dishes. Spoon the sauce over each dish.

DEEP-FRIED TOFU WITH DASHI SAUCE [AGEDASHI-DOFU]

This dish is very easy to make, but makes a great accompany of the cooked rice. The important tip is not to drain the tofu too much, and not to heat up the frying oil too much. Those two are the things I always care. Only thing to bother you is grating daikon radish; it takes a lot of work, so you may need to do in advance. The dish is so good when eating while it's hot.

SAUTÉED EGGPLANT & GREEN PEPPERS WITH SWEET MISO

The sweet miso sauce goes especially well with the flavor of the fried eggplant, and I love it paired with a bowl of rice. Growing up, my mother made it often at my request, and now I make it frequently for my family. It's a versatile dish that can be changed by adding ground beef, sliced pork or green onions according to your taste.

TOFU AND MENTAIKO AU GRATIN

Mentaiko is spicy haddock roe marinated in umami seasonings. Originally a Korean ingredient, it has become one of the most popular accompaniments for rice in Japan. It has also been used to develop unique recipes like spaghetti with mentaiko sauce, and this dish is another example of this creativity. You could also add a layer of cooked macaroni to create a satisfying side dish to meat.

SHIITAKE TSUKUDANI

Tukudani is a type of pickle made by simmering vegetables in a soy sauce mixture. It can be served as a small appetizer or side dish as well as incorporated into sushi rolls, chirashi sushi, and sushi pockets (*inari-zushi*).

EGGPLANT IN DASHI

Maybe you've never experienced how delicious simmered eggplant can be. They absorb the flavorful stock and seasoning and become smooth and tender. This dish is great served warm, but it's also refreshing when chilled and served as a midsummer snack.

DEEP-FRIED TOFU
WITH DASHI SAUCE [AGEDASHI-DOFU] ▸ Serves 4

1 block *momen* tofu or firm tofu, about
    300 g / 11 oz.
Flour, for dredging
Vegetable oil, for deep frying

Sauce:
    100 ml dashi
    1 Tablespoon mirin
    1 ½ Tablespoons soy sauce

5-cm / 2-in long piece of daikon,
    peeled and grated
1 heaping tablespoon grated ginger

4 sweet, mild chili peppers,
    pierced in several places with a
    toothpick

I Wrap the block of tofu with paper towels. Place between two boards and allow to drain for about 10 minutes.

2 Combine the sauce ingredients in a pan. As soon as mixture reaches a boil, remove from the heat.

3 Cut the Tofu into 4 pieces and toss with the flour to coat evenly. Deep fry in 170°C / 340°F oil until light brown and crispy. Drain on a paper towel. Deep fry the peppers (without any coating) in the same oil for 5 seconds.

4 Place the tofu in a serving dish and pour some of the hot sauce over the top. Garnish with the grated daikon and ginger.

SAUTÉED EGGPLANT &
GREEN PEPPERS WITH SWEET MISO ▸ Serves 4

4 Japanese eggplants
3 small green bell peppers or *piiman*
    (sweet and slightly bitter green
    peppers)
2 Tablespoons sesame oil

Sweet miso (Mixed in advance):
    2 Tablespoons miso,
      preferably yellow
    1 Tablespoon sugar
    2 Tablespoons mirin
    1 Tablespoon sake

I Remove the tops from the eggplants. Cut each in half lengthwise first, then and crosswise into 1-cm / ½ -in. thick pieces. Soak in water for 10 minutes to remove bitterness. Drain well.

2 Remove the tops from the bell peppers, cut each in half lengthwise, remove seeds, and cut each half into approximately 2-cm / 1-in. pieces.

3 Add the sesame oil to a frying pan and heat over medium heat. Add the eggplant and fry until they begin to soften. Add the green peppers and fry a few more minutes.

4 Add the sweet miso sauce and stir until the liquid in the pan has almost entirely evaporated. Arrange into a serving plate.

TOFU AND MENTAIKO AU GRATIN ▸ Serves 4

Mentaiko béchamel sauce:
   3 large lobes of mentaiko
   150 g/ 5 ½ oz. tofu, well-drained
      and cut into 8-mm/ ⅓ -in thick
      slices
      *See p.17 for draining pro-
      cedure.

   3 Tablespoons butter
   3 Tablespoons flour
   300 ml milk, room temperature

1 potato, steamed and cut into
     8-mm / ⅓-in. thick slices
Shredded pizza cheese

1 For the mentaiko béchamel sauce: Make a long slit in the center of each mentaiko lobe, cut open, and scrape out the roe using the back of a knife. Set aside. Melt the butter in a frying pan over low heat. Stir in the flour and mix until smooth. Add the milk in small batches, whisking with each addition until it is completely incorporated. Mix in the mentaiko.

2 Spread ⅓ of the mentaiko béchamel sauce in the bottom of an oven-proof dish. Layers the sliced potato, ⅓ of the sauce, the sliced tofu and then the remainder of the sauce. Cover the top with shredded cheese.

3 Bake in a 250°C / 475°F oven for 15 minutes, or until the top is nicely browned.

SHIITAKE TSUKUDANI ▸ Serves 4

5 dried shiitake mushrooms,
   reconstituted in water
   in the refrigerator for 24 hours
1 ½ Tablespoons sugar
1 Tablespoon mirin
1 Tablespoon soy sauce
150 ml shiitake dashi*
   *Measure the reconstituting water
   from the shiitake mushrooms,
   and add water if it is less than
   150 ml

Remove the hard stems from the shiitake and cut the caps into strips. Place the shiitake, sugar, mirin, soy sauce, and shiitake stock in a saucepan over medium heat and bring to a simmer. Cook until the liquid nearly evaporates. Let it cool in the room temperature. It keeps 1 month in an air tight container in the refrigerator.

EGGPLANT IN DASHI ▸ Serves 4

4 Japanese eggplants

Simmering liquid:
   400 ml dashi
   3 Tablespoons sake
   1 ½ Tablespoons sugar
   3 Tablespoons soy sauce

20 g / ⅔ oz. ginger, grated

1 Remove the tops from the eggplants and cut each in half length wise. Make multiple thin slits on the skin and soak in water for 10 minutes.

2 Combine the simmering liquid ingredients in a saucepan and heat until warm. Add the eggplants, skin-side down, cover and cook for 5 minutes. Flip the eggplants, cover, and cook for 5 to 10 minutes, or until tender.

3 Remove from the heat and flip the eggplants so that they are skin-side down to prevent discoloration. Allow to cool slightly.

4 Arrange the eggplants on a plate along with some of the simmering liquid, and garnish with grated ginger.

6

RICE
&
SOUP

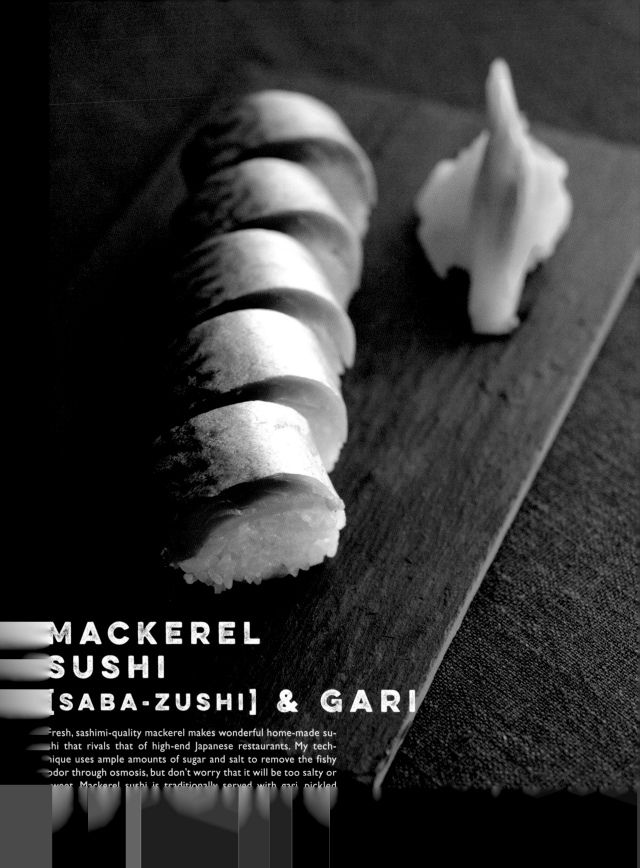

MACKEREL SUSHI
[SABA-ZUSHI] & GARI

Fresh, sashimi-quality mackerel makes wonderful home-made sushi that rivals that of high-end Japanese restaurants. My technique uses ample amounts of sugar and salt to remove the fishy
odor through osmosis, but don't worry that it will be too salty or
sweet. Mackerel sushi is traditionally served with gari, pickled

MACKEREL SUSHI [SABA-ZUSHI] ▸ Serves 4

1 whole sashimi-quality mackerel
   (or 2 fillets of mackerel)
2 handfuls of sugar
2 handfuls of sea salt
Rice vinegar
Gari (see below for recipe)

Seasoned rice, made from 180 ml uncooked
   short-grain rice (see p.31 for recipe)

1 Fillet the mackerel. (You don't need to remove bones and skins yet). Use a tray that easily holds the two fillets. Sprinkle the bottom of the tray with a handful of sugar, place the fillets skin-side down on it, and sprinkle the fillets with another handful of sugar. Allow to sit for 30 minutes in the refrigerator to remove the fishy odor.

2 Rinse the fillets in water, and pat dry with paper towels.

3 Sprinkle a clean tray with a generous amount of salt, lightly covering the entire bottom. Lightly sprinkle the fillets with another handful salt, just covering the surface of the fish. You may use less salt on thin parts like the tail portion. Allow to cure for an hour and half in the refrigerator.

4 Rinse the fillets in water, and pat dry with paper towels.

5 Place the fillets on a clean tray, add the vinegar to barely cover the fillets, and allow to marinate for 10 minutes in the refrigerator. Flip and let it marinate in the refrigerator for another 10 minutes.

6 Wipe the vinegar from the fillets. Remove the belly bones with a knife and pick out the pin bones with bone tweezers. Pinch the opaque thin skin near the head and carefully peel the skin down to the tail side.

7 Line a sushi mat with a plastic wrap, and place one fillet skin-side down. Spread some of gari and half of the seasoned rice on top, roll tightly, and secure the roll with rubber bands at the top, bottom, and center, keeping the sushi mat wrapped on the outside. Repeat with the other fillet, and allow them to sit to secure for about an hour.

8 Unwrap, and cut into desired thickness using a moist knife.

GARI

Marinade:
   200 ml rice vinegar
   3 to 4 Tablespoons sugar
   1 teaspoon salt

200 g / 7 oz. fresh ginger, preferably new
   crop
Salt

1 Place the marinade ingredients in a non-reactive saucepan and bring to a simmer. Remove from the heat and allow to cool.

2 With skin on, use a vegetable peeler or slicer to cut the ginger into thin strips. Sprinkle with salt, mix, and allow to sit for 5 minutes.

3 Bring a large amount of water to a boil in a medium saucepan, blanch the ginger slices for a few minutes. Remove the slices using a perforated ladle, drain well, and immediately add them to the marinade.

4 Transfer the sliced ginger with the marinade into a clean, air-tight container, and let it marinate for 2 to 5 days.

*If you pickle myoga along with the ginger, the gari will take on an even brighter pink hue. Cut each myoga in half lengthwise, sprinkle with salt, and blanch before adding to the marinade with the ginger.

STUFFED SQUID WITH GLUTENOUS RICE [IKAMESHI]

This is a classic bento lunch that's a local specialty in my mother's hometown of Hokkaido. Some people find squid to be rubbery. But when stuffed with glutinous rice, the squid transforms and becomes more tender.

MISO SOUP WITH TOFU & WAKAME

Miso soups is especially delicious with the addition of two or three seasonal ingredients. Most of my students had only tasted instant dashi stock which is full of additives, so they are surprised when they taste real home-made miso soup, full of natural umami, for the first time. And each time I see their reaction, I think about how it doesn't matter where you come from, everyone loves comfort food.

OYAKI DUMPLINGS

Oyaki is a local specialty in Nagano, which is a beautiful mountainous prefecture. These are seared and steamed dumplings and the extra steps create the ideal texture, much like well-baked sourdough bread. As for the filling, anything goes. Here I'll introduce two types, one sweet and one savory. I always make large batches and freeze them to have on hand for a quick snack.

KENCHIN VEGAN SOUP

This soup is believed to have originated from the Kenchin Temple in Kamakura, known for its practice of Zen Buddhism. Though the recipe contains only plant foods it includes some cooking tips to make it satisfying such as using oil and combinations of particular ingredients. In this case, "dashi" refers to kombu or shiitake. For a non-vegan version, use regular dashi or chicken stock.

STUFFED SQUID
WITH GLUTENOUS RICE [IKAMESHI]
▸ Makes 2 stuffed squid

2 dried shiitake mushrooms,
    reconstituted in about a cup
    of water in the refrigerator
    for 24 hours
    *Reserve the reconstituting water
    (shiitake dashi)
200 ml dry glutenous rice,
    soaked in water in the refrigerator
    overnight
4 squid, about 20 cm / 8 in. long
5-cm / 2-in. long piece of carrot

Seasoning A:
    2 Tablespoons sake
    2 Tablespoons mirin
    2 Tablespoons soy sauce

Seasoning B:
    800 ml shiitake water
    *Measure the reconstituting
    water from the shiitake mush-
    rooms, and add water to make
    800 ml
    100 ml sake
    4 Tablespoons mirin
    4 Tablespoons soy sauce
    3 ½ Tablespoons sugar

1 Clean the squid, removing all of the innards. Separate the body and the tentacles and pat dry. Cut the tentacles into 1-cm / ½ -in. pieces and blanch in boiling water for a few seconds.

2 Cut the carrot into thin strips. Cut off the hard stems from the reconstituted mushrooms and thinly slice the caps. Drain the rice.

3 In a medium bowl, combine the carrot, mushrooms, and rice with all of the ingredients of Seasoning A.

4 Stuff each squid with the rice mixture, about 70% full, leaving space in the body cavity for the rice to expand during cooking. Secure the squid with a toothpick to close the cavity, leaving a 1 to 2 cm / ½ to 1 in. margin from the bottom.

5 Bring all of the ingredients of Seasoning B to a boil in a large stock pot. Add the stuffed squid, cover with a drop-lid, and let them simmer for about an hour and half. As the end of the cooking time approaches, check whether rice is cooked by poking it with a skewer. If the rice is not yet cooked but there is not much cooking liquid in the pan, add some water or dashi.

6 Slice the stuffed squid into 1 to 1.5-cm / ½-in. thick rounds, wetting the knife before each cut.

MISO SOUP WITH TOFU & WAKAME ▸ Serves 4

½ block tofu, 200 g / 7 oz.
30 g / 1 oz. salt-preserved wakame
    (*enzo-wakmae*)
4 Tablespoons yellow miso
600 ml dashi

1 Cover the wakame with enough water to keep it submerged for 5 minutes or according to the package instructions. Rinse in water, drain, dry with paper towels, and cut into bite-sized pieces. Cut the tofu into small cubes.

2 Place the dashi and tofu in a pot over medium heat, and when the tofu is heated through, turn off the heat. Add the wakame pieces. Dissolve the miso gradually.

3 Serve in individual bowls.

OYAKI DUMPLINGS ▸ Makes 8 dumplings

Dough:
    200 g / 7 oz. all purpose flour
    140 ml hot water
    A pinch salt

Squash filling:
    200 g / 7 oz. kabocha squash,
        steamed and peeled
    2 Tablespoons sugar

Eggplant filling:
    Half of Sautéed Eggplants
        and Bell Peppers with Sweet
        Miso Recipe (see p.65)

Vegetable oil for searing dumplings

1 To make the dough, combine hot water and salt in a bowl and mix with cooking chopsticks. Add the flour and mix well. When the dough has cooled enough to barely touch, knead the on a work surface by hand for several minutes. Cover with plastic wrap and let it stand at room temperature for about 30 minutes.
2 Combine the steamed squash with sugar, divide into quarters, and make four balls. Drain the eggplant filling if needed, and divide into four parts.
3 Divide the dough into 8 pieces, make each into a ball, and flatten into circles, each 10 cm / 4 in. in diameter. Place the divided fillings in the center of the circle, wrap, and seal by twisting the top. (You may want to place the dumplings sealed side down. Also, cover the dough or dumplings with plastic wrap as you work to prevent them from drying out.)
4 Heat 1 teaspoon of vegetable oil at a time in a frying pan, add the dumplings sealed side down first, and sear the both sides. Work in small batches so as not to overcrowd the pan.
5 Steam the dumplings for 10 minutes so that the center is heated through.

*You can first steam and then sear the dumplings for a more crispy exterior.

KENCHIN VEGAN SOUP ▸ Serves 4

½ block tofu, 200 g / 7 oz.,
    drained and cut into cubes
1 sheet *abura-age* (fried tofu pouch),
    cut into short strips
4 *satoimo* (Japanese taro roots)
5-cm / 2-in. long piece of daikon
¼ carrot
¼ burdock root
1 Tablespoon sesame oil
600 ml kombu dashi or shiitake dashi
½ Japanese long onion (*naganegi*),
    chopped
2 Tablespoons soy sauce
1 Tablespoon mirin
* 3 to 4 tablespoons of miso can be substituted in place of the soy sauce and mirin.

1 Peel satoimo taro roots, place in a pan with cold water, and bring to a boil. Cook for 5 minutes and rinse in cold water.
2 Peel the daikon and carrot, quarter lengthwise, and cut each into thin slices.
3 Brush off any dirt from the gobo under running water, and shape into thin strips using a knife.
4 Heat the sesame oil in a saucepan, add the taro, daikon, carrot, and abura-age tofu pouch pieces, bring to a simmer, and cook for about 5 minutes. Add the dashi and tofu, simmer, and cook until all the root vegetables become tender.
5 Add the chopped onion, soy sauce, and mirin, and simmer for 5 minutes.
6 Serve in individual serving bowls.

FAVORITE STORES
IN TSUKIJI MARKET

The small retail shops in Tsukiji remain some of my favorite places to shop,
even after the relocation of the Tsukiji Central Wholesale Market.
This area, called Tsukiji *Jogai* (meaning "outside of the market") can get
quite crowded so I prefer shopping early in the morning.

KOMBU

Kotobukiya Shouten

Vendors of kombu for over 200 years, they sell a wide range of ingredients for making Japanese stocks, including kombu for every-day use to connoisseur-grade kombu used in high-end restaurants. Stepping into the store away from the crowds on the street, it's fun just to look at the variety of kombu hanging on the wall.

4-13-6, Tsukiji, Chuo-ku, Tokyo
Phone: 03-3542-8981
Open Hours: 6am – 2pm
Closed: Sundays, holidays, and when tsukiji central wholesale market is closed
http://www.kotobuki-ya.biz/

MEAT

Oumiya Meat Shop

This meat purveyor was founded in Tokyo over 80 years ago by its president who trained in Oumi, an area famous for its Wa-gyu production. Their beef and pork are the freshest in the area. I also love their sweet-salty chao shao, a type of Chinese-style charcuterie which is you can snack while walking down the street.

4-14-1, Tsukiji, Chuo-ku, Tokyo
Phone: 03-3541-7398
Open Hours: 6am – 2:30pm
Closed: Sundays, holidays, and when tsukiji central wholesale market is closed
http://tsukiji-oumiya.co.jp

POULTRY

Toritoh

Like other small stores in the Tsukiji area, this specialized poultry shop sells the fresh-est chicken and duck to professionals as well as novice cooks. At the front of the shop they sell ready-to-eat karaage fried chicken and smoked chicken, and people form long lines for these street snacks. They also have a casual restaurant serving a variety of chicken and rice bowls nearby.

4-10-18, Tsukiji, Chuo-ku, Tokyo
Phone: 03-3541-2545
Open Hours: 5am – 1pm
Closed: Sundays, holidays, and when tsukiji central wholesale market is closed
http://www.toritoh.com/

NORI

Maruyama Nori-ten

As you step into the shop, you may be sur-prised by the wide variety of nori. Whether it's for making rolled sushi or using as a topping, here you'll find something that meets your needs. They also carry select green teas and supply high-end sushi res-taurants with their products.

4-7-5, Tsukiji, Chuo-ku, Tokyo
Phone: 03-3541-0223
Open Hours: 7:30am – 6pm
Closed: Sundays and holidays
http://www.maruyamanori.com/

WHEAT GLUTEN CAKES[OFU]

Kakuyama Honten

Specializing in fresh "fu", wheat gluten cakes, they have carried on the tradition of making Edo-style fu (*tsuto-fu*) for many years. They also make excellent and high-quality yuba, tofu skin.

6-21-1, Tsukiji, Chuou-ku, Tokyo
Phone: 03-3541-8141
Open Hours: 5:30am – 2pm
Closed: Sundays, holidays, and when tsukiji central wholesale market is closed
http://www.kakuyama.net/

DRIED BEANS

Shiota Shoten

I'm always excited to see the variety of dried beans they offer at this shop. Just tak-ing kidney beans as an example, they have numerous varieties harvested from differ-ent growing regions. Because of the selec-tion they offer, I find myself experimenting and trying varieties that are new to me.

4-14-12, Tsukiji, Chuo-ku, Tokyo
Phone: 03-3541-0640
Open Hours: 5am – 2pm
Closed: Sundays, holidays, and when Tsukiji central wholesale market is closed

MARI NAMESHIDA

A professional home cook well-versed in many cuisines—from Kaiseki and Shojin to French—Mari began teaching home-style cooking classes in her Tokyo kitchen in 2011. At *Cooking with Mari*, located near the Tsukiji market, her students are able to experience the real food culture of Japan, one which doesn't transpire in restaurants. Fluent in English, Mandarin, and Japanese, she teaches upwards of 100 students each month from around the world. Trip Advisor recently selected *Cooking with Mari* as the number one culinary activity in the Tokyo area.

撮影／山家 学

スタイリング／岩﨑牧子

アートディレクション／細山田光宣（細山田デザイン事務所）

デザイン／藤井保奈（細山田デザイン事務所）

ヘアメイク／半田知也

取材・文・翻訳／横田典子

翻訳／ケリー・ワルドロン

編集／河合知子

撮影協力／
釜浅商店 ☎03-3841-9355
　（P.12南部寄せ鍋24cm、P.51釜浅の鉄打ち出しフライパン20cm）
UTUWA ☎03-6447-0070
AWABEES ☎03-5786-1600

JAPANESE RECIPES FROM MARI'S TOKYO KITCHEN

2015年8月30日　初版第1刷発行

著者	滑志田真理
編集長	大木淳夫
発行人	木本敬巳
発行・発売	ぴあ株式会社
	〒150-0011
	東京都渋谷区東1-2-20 渋谷ファーストタワー
	編集　☎03-5774-5267
	販売　☎03-5774-5248
印刷・製本	大日本印刷株式会社